# The Beautiful Inventions

By the same author

*Poetry*
**Fairground Music**
**The Tree that Walked**
**Cannibals and Missionaries**
**Epistles to Several Persons**
**The Mountain in the Sea**
**Lies and Secrets**
**The Illusionists** *A Tale*

*Criticism*
**A Reader's Guide to W.H. Auden**
**The Sonnet**

*For children*
**Herod Do Your Worst**
**Squeaking Crust**
**The Spider Monkey Uncle King**
**A Bestiary**
**The Last Bid**
**The Extraordinary Wool Mill and other stories**

# The Beautiful Inventions

# John Fuller

Secker & Warburg
London

First published in England 1983 by
Martin Secker & Warburg Limited
54 Poland Street, London W1V 3DF

Copyright © John Fuller 1983

British Library Cataloguing in Publication Data

Fuller, John, 1937—
    The Beautiful Inventions.
    I. Title
    821'.914      PR6056.U43

    ISBN 0-436-16811-1

SUBSIDISED BY THE
**Arts Council**
OF GREAT BRITAIN

Printed in Great Britain by
Redwood Burn Limited
Trowbridge

# Contents

## Acknowledgements

Acknowledgements are due to the following, in which some of these poems first appeared: BBC Radio 3, *Encounter, A Florilegium for John Florio* (Sycamore Press), *Harper's and Queen, The January Divan* (Mandeville Press), *Observer Colour Magazine, Outposts, PEN Broadsheet, Penguin Book of Light Verse, Poetry Book Society Christmas Supplement, Poetry (Hong Kong), Poetry Review, Quarto, Sunday Times, Times Literary Supplement.*
"Linda" was commissioned by the Reading Phoenix Choir and performed in a setting by Bryan Kelly at the opening of the Reading Hexagon in 1977.

# Retreat

I should like to live in a sunny town like this
Where every afternoon is half-day closing
And I would wait at the terminal for the one train
Of the day, pacing the platform, and no one arriving.

At the far end of the platform is a tunnel, and the train
Slows out of it like a tear from a single eye.
You couldn't get further than this, the doors all opened
And the porter with rolled sleeves wielding a mop.

Even if one restless traveller were to arrive
With leather grip, racquets under the arm,
A belted raincoat folded over the shoulder,
A fishing hat, and a pipe stuck in his mouth,

There would be nowhere for him to move on to
And he would settle down to tea in the lounge
Of the Goat Hotel, doing yesterday's crossword,
And would emerge later, after a nap, for a drink.

You meet them in the bar, glassy-eyed, all the time.
They never quite unpack, and expect letters
From one particular friend who doesn't write.
If you buy them a drink they will tell you their life history:

"I should have liked to live in a sunny town like this,
Strolling down to the harbour in the early evening,
Looking at the catch. Nothing happens here.
You could forget the ill-luck dogging you.

"I could join the Fancy Rat Society and train
Sweet peas over the trellised porch
Of my little slice of stuccoed terrace. I could
Be in time for the morning service at Tesco's.

"I expect death's like this, letters never arriving
And the last remembered failure at once abandoned
And insistent, like a card on a mantelpiece.
What might it be? You can take your choice.

" 'I shook her by the shoulders in a rage of frustration.'
'I smiled, and left the room without saying a word.'
'I was afraid to touch her, and never explained.'
'I touched her once, and that was my greatest mistake.' "

You meet them before dinner. You meet them after dinner,
The unbelieved, the uncaressed, the terrified.
Their conversation is perfectly decent but usually
It slows to a halt and they start to stare into space.

You would like it here. Life is quite ordinary
And the self-pity oozes into the glass like bitters.
What's your poison? Do you have a desire to drown?
We're all in the same boat. Join us. Feel free.

And when the bar closes we can say good-bye
And make our way to the terminal where the last
(Or is it the first?) train of the day is clean and waiting
To take us slowly back to where we came from.

But will we ever return? Who needs us now?
It's the town that requires us, though the streets are empty.
It's become a habit and a retreat. Or a form of justice.
Living in a sunny town like this.

## Year of the Child

Furiously behind its frozen lens
The shutter moves. And catches the breath
That will not live to cloud it.

Winter has hugged the world to death
And still the shutter moves, a thin
Turnstile for populations.

Eyes stare at the eyes staring
Forever unblinking, the paper is printed
And the shutter is still moving.

Moving and not moved, the eyes close
And the paper recreates hunger
Like inflated currency.

We must believe it, for our anger
Is blown about the world, a ransom
Refused. The shutter moves:

Over the year's grave, and the child's,
One by one a million shutters
Darken just for a moment.

We seek the selfhood of the race
In the shared turbulence of beauty
That creates the human face.

And that face is winter. Is nothing.
Is our bad understanding. Is uncreated.
And the shutter is still.

10

# Topkapi

I am the sultan. Jewelled, I sit on jewels.
My head bows with the weight of jewels.
My fingers curl open with the weight of jewels.

They bring me a bowl of emeralds the size of figs
To play with if I want to, and curds
To eat with spoons so diamonded
They rasp my lower lip.

I have a candlestick
With 6666 diamonds. The British Queen
Has sent me the jewelled order of her garter.

One day I will throw myself into the Bosphorus.

## Sultan Ahmet Square

In Sultan Ahmet Square
The brass domes of the pots
In the boot-boy's box
Echo the domes of the mosque
On which one seems to step
As if to threaten Blefuscu
While on the leather are mixed
The browns and blues and blacks
That would let a Whistler daub
A dissimilar sky to the sky
From which now Allah leans
To admire his shining toe-caps.

## Fuatpaşa Caddesi

On Fuatpaşa Caddesi
A man stands all day in the mud
With ten bedsteads against a railing.
They are for sale, but no one buys.

Down Çadircilar Caddesi
A man staggers as though inspecting the mud
With ten mattresses roped to his back.
He is taking them somewhere from somewhere else.

In the evening they drink warm salep by the bridge
And the cinnamon tickles their throats!

## Galata Bridge

They stand patiently in doorways
Fingering their rifles like exhibitionists.
Eyes are averted from bayonets.
Crowds pass busily, resigned like brides.

They are required to look serious in case
Anyone pauses long enough to laugh,
And because their upper lips are shaven,
Leaving them vulnerable and naked.

There is a tank by the Galata Bridge
Which has not come down the steep streets
Nor over the bridge, which rocks in frail sections
That let through the dawn shipping.

It is positioned here mysteriously
Angled on its concrete eminence,
As though by a boy kneeling with a toy,
Breathing heavily, placing it exactly.

## Mosque

One hand keeps a scarf to the mouth, the other
Holds the paired shoes lightly at waist level
Like the violinist's finishing flourish of the bow,
The eyes looking down in modesty and concentration.

Carpets layer the stone, careless, unstinting.
A patch of window shows rain, and a ship passing.
The dome muffles whispers like a yawn, and on
The grandfather clock are numerals like closed umbrellas.

Outside, the rituals of trade and government
Continue to gather and disperse the organisms
Which here have no place in the everlasting designs
That weave their studied intervals around you.

Except for a few flowers you may warily tread on
As you walk further and further into the silence
Or find repeated in the baked gardens of the walls
That reach their blue and orange to the dome.

Prayer

Prayer is talking to these beautiful inventions
And is agreed to be a performance
Best conducted in a professional silence.

Beneath the great hanging circles of lamps
On the rich carpets they settle themselves
And begin to practise their headstands.

Don't we recognise the pretence
From our own feinted applause?

**St Sophia**

Two figures there beneath the dome, walking with similar pace,
Turned as the other turned, forward and back, in that empty
                                                        space.

Turning on the heel, looking about, casual but intense,
With everything that might belong to a stranger's cautious
                                                        grace.

Eyes like hands went out to the marble and stone and precise
                                                        gold
On the walls where the guarding images left a broken trace.

In the narthex, in the galleries, in the side-aisles,
Up and down, as drawn to each other as to that echoing place.

As though it were the whole world, and I saw the man was
                                                        myself
And he walked there with the woman and the woman had
                                                        your face.

## Çiçek Pasaji

Here on the dirty edge of everything
The streets are dark, pleasure uncertain.
But the fish and flowers are bright
As the loud throats of the stallkeepers!

Pipes of bones, and wigs and shawls of tripes;
Fish like wet embryos of fallen angels
Head down or gills unhinged
Caught by a beneficent fisherman
At some willed apocalyptic abortion
Of all the other world; lights behind glass;
Tulips on fire; spices bright as pigments;
Hissing of cooking; globes of oranges;
Our tight fingers, interlaced in wool.

And-in dark alleys, a flickering bucket,
The hopeful outcast's fire.

## Being

Being not elsewhere now
I wouldn't want to be
    Other than here,
With wine still in the glass,
Watching the year pass.

Being not yet asleep,
The fire glowing steady
    And furred with ash,
I take what was meant,
Receive what was sent.

Being is a wish,
Tilting the final inch
    Against the glow,
That being, once removed,
Need never more be proved.

Being, though, as cold
As it surely will be,
    Proof will be pointless:
Better to treat with caution
The planetary portion.

---

## Variation on Gautier

This black dress: it gives me joy
To see you in it, the cut of the shoulder
The arms in repose, the hidden bosom,
Naked the pagan throat and chin!

The quilted pensiveness of beauty
Lies in the soft touch of the stuff:
I would not wish a conspiracy
Of any other compelling textures.

Not the severity of shame
Colours this formal fabric: no,
It is the chastity of art
That veils in dreams the frank and nude.

Its deep shadows are the attentions
Of many unappeased desires
Which attract to the body that denies them
The vestments of a secret devouring!

# Ironing

## 1 *Handkerchiefs*

They are impressed, imposed in 16mo
And lastly collated, the fingers walking up
Their ladder of warm cotton corners like money.

Later, when they are needed, they are carefully opened
And stared at, as though counterfeit, in the frozen
Instantaneous disbelief of a sneeze.

## 2 *Jeans*

The board is hard between their legs
As they cling in abject fear of being
Thrown. Endurance is an ignominy,
Branded on the bum by a gothic arch.

## 3 *Shirts*

Collars crease into smiles, the weak armpits
Are tickled and the empty wrists hang limply.
The heat relaxes and the stroking appeases
The possible flap and flutter of spooky sleeves.

There are mornings when we bound upstairs
And open their coffins simply to establish
That they are still lying in peaceable folds
Under pungent sachets of prophylactic herbs.

How may we exorcize them? Mirrors reflect
The innocent idiot smirk of a confident victim
Careless of their guile which requires him to tighten
The fatal noose around his own neck, too.

# A Mysterious Present

Two bottles lifted chilled
From their shredded paper duvets
    With Gilpin clink,
Not the less rare
For travelling as a pair.

A face with white moustaches
Medallioned on their bosoms
    Gravely presides
An inch above the label
Where they stand on the table:

Gruaud-Larose, a fine
St Julien, its sobered
    Purple enclosed
In white and black and gold,
A dozen years old.

Good for a dozen glasses
Among four friends, with talk
    Of nothing much,
And guesses at who sent
Such a distinguished present.

Loyal companions, braced
And knowing each other's secrets!
    Where one goes
The other, hearing laughter,
Will gladly follow after.

**Steamed Carps' Cheeks**

How shall we find carps' cheeks
Without some monkish slaughter?
Visions of fallen angels
Puffing through stagnant water
And rising to the chant
Of hungry pious brothers!
Well, if certain fish
Are strangers, there are others:
In Oxford Cattle Market
On a Wednesday morning
At eight o'clock, suppressing
Your instinctive yawning
(Is that what cheeks are for?)
Go with your wife and look
At the stall where what they sell
Is caught by net and hook.
There you will find cods' cheeks
Which to my mind will do,
And at sixty pence a pound
Are cheap enough to chew.
Take them home and soak them
In a quantity of sherry
(Though they'd use something stronger,
I guess, in that monastery).
Add sliced ginger and
Mushroom (if your grocer
Has Chinese, buy it — or
Pholliota squarrosa
Which grows around trees —
Or if you cannot find
Such fragrant fungus use
The ordinary kind).
Season the fish and line
A bowl with sesame oil.

Put the whole lot in,
Cover with silver foil
And steam for about an hour.
It is a dish that brings
Happy reflective thoughts
Of aqueous sleepy things.

## Black Pudding

Butter a hot pan and therein slice,
Thumb-thick, a whole black quoit
Of black pudding. Add half a dozen lean
Rashers, cut to the size of the side
Of a box of matches; two large Bramleys
In chunks; and stir. The pudding's purple,
Flecked with white, blackens as you turn it
Until it shines with fat, a winning set
Of draughts. The bacon shrinks and crisps.
Before the apple does much more than soften
Add a whole tin of anchovies, each cut
In three. Stir once again, and serve.
Afterwards you may walk the block,
Or collect your daughter from judo, noticing
In the jut of lip and foot in the jostling
For a fall, an equal determination.
Then coffee, and music. And perhaps a cigar.

## Sorrel

Apologies to the snail
For gathering his dinner
    And perhaps tomorrow's,
With whom I have no quarrel
As fingers search for sorrel.

The leaves are stacked against
The thumb, ready to spring
    Apart again
As from the packed plastic
They dump their green elastic

And stir upon the table,
A dark dealt freshness,
    In gathered mounds
Of vegetable life
That moisten to the knife.

With butter in a pan
They fall to a khaki slime
    As sharp as a lemon.
Outside, it continues to rain
And the snails walk again.

## Wasp Nest

Be careful not to crush
This scalloped tenement:
Who knows what secrets
Winter has failed to find
Within its paper walls?

It is the universe
Looking entirely inwards,
A hanging lantern
Whose black light wriggles
Through innumerable chambers

Where hopes still sleep
In her furry pews,
The chewed dormitory
Of a forgotten tribe
That layered its wooden pearl.

It is a basket of memories,
A museum of dead work,
The spat Babel of summer
With a marvellous language
Of common endeavour.

Note: it is the fruit
Returning to the tree,
The world becoming a clock
For sleep, a matrix of pure
Energy, a book of many lives.

## Humming Bird

Blurred bright thing!
Most curious
Behaviour of
A dying planet!

Immobile as
A star we know
Has moved and will,
Hovering

Over the hot
Vegetation,
Alert and alerting
The observer

Like a footnote
Asterisked
To a cancelled
Paragraph.

Still the inert
World of matter
Reminds it of
Its origins.

A flower mocks
Its stolen colour
And is siphoned
For energy.

Everything spinning
Up and away!
The globe is drained
Into the air!

## Zuni Owl

Squat owl pot with umber ears
And painted eyes, your wings alert
But thumbed down to comic handles,
The posture ruffled but dignified!

Your lip and phallic nose droop
To hide your only orifice
Noiseless when blown and just too small
To welcome liquids or reveal

The hurt spirit hiding there,
That lifetime's guardian in his break-
able body of earth, waiting for our
Forgetfulness, and his release.

# Small

Small wit, small will,
Small call, small kill,
Small flight, small fall,
Small say, small small.

Small love, small lies,
Small purse, small prize,
Small view, small verse,
Small what, small worse.

**Signs**

Talking to animals? The animal novel?
To hell with the stable ego of gorilla!
We look for signs. And she does sign,
Though with a dark air of abstractedness.
"Beans hurry give me beans."
O lovely behaviour of silksad gorilla!
Is coal or soot, immortal coal or soot!

## Old Things

The nest in the sycamore has outlasted
The night's wind, but was already
Empty, its twigs just as unuseful
As these on the lawn of the morning's damage,
Its role bizarre, challenging, symbolic,
Like a crown in a bush on a battlefield.

The old barometer has traced
The wind's descent on its cylinder
Of paper, the loops of ink lapping
Its chequered weeks like a prize miler,
The information, required or not,
Accumulating under the glass.

These things stir the heart with regret
For all our fruitless struggles and hopes,
The lost chances, the hoarded rubbish.

# Uncertainties

These moments of waiting
For an unarranged meeting
Are full of the strangest uncertainties
As the mind delightedly shifts in its willing vertigo.

Imagine a book deciding
Upon this or that meaning
In that close second before you open it,
The loose print tumbling together, the hand on the doorknob!

What will be, will be.
Everything has its way.
What did you expect from the encounter?
Did you think your life would be changed like the end of a
chapter?

Decision is a failing
To understand feeling,
How it responds eagerly to the response.
Books are beautiful but dead. Who is reading whom?

Or perhaps the event's reversal
Was designed by rehearsal
And the future is simply the tide you swim with
Turning page after page after page after page after page.

## The Wood

This wood is not a wood to hide in.
It is a place to run about in,
A place where both the shoulders show
At once and the thin trees inclining
One to the other make tangled arches
That you must brush aside as you pass.

Where you stop, six ladybirds
As it might be hibernating
In a tree's armpit. Each pair
Of wing-cases as closely folded
As the stiff glass and gold leaves
Of an old time-piece, not going.

Have you looked up and seen something
Disappearing that was not a branch
Or the quick bird that left it nodding,
Curious for buds? Something that left
The grey and violet air more conscious
Of the still space it occupied?

If you do run, the dead trees
Stirring in broken sleep beneath you,
All you do is find yourself
In a different part of the same wood.
And no one seeing you can be sure
That they have seen you. And no one is there.

## Primrose

With one knee arched over the ditch,
Finger and thumb reaching for the base of the stem,
I can't recall what the word was I'd forgotten.

Perhaps it was something the heart thought,
Loud in its cave of blood. If so, no matter.
I know I'll remember. Perhaps when I least want to.

For now the flower speaks in my hand.
The deep yellow at its centre melts to the petals,
A perfect wash. Its memory is in its face.

## Absence

What can the world worse arrange
Than its encounters in time and place?
Imagine a girl taking her horse
Towards the sun. Frowning slightly,
She pushes back the hair from her eyes.

A walker, striding with cut switch
The length of a cropped valley, the wind
Just strong enough for new lambs
To lean into, finds nothing to swing at
Except a patch of opening gorse.

When an Easter butterfly
Weaves out of it, giddy with hope,
His gloom is complete. There on the sward
Are clustered the shallow clear mud-ghosts
Of horseshoes. Which might be hers. But aren't.

## Secrets

Secrets certainly have a power to charm.
In front of you, an ape; behind, a chasm.
Keep it happy, keep it happy! Its fangs are hideous!
You must be almost a day's trek from your hideout!
A secret will make it pause. A secret amuses.
Take off your skin. Do explorers have anuses?
What a joke! Show it the other hole,
The metal one. Bang. The point goes home.

Elsewhere, secrets have greater pathos:
Flushed wives prepare themselves on patios,
Guilt an excuse for talk. After eight
The appeasing Bacardi develops into a fight.
But see them next morning, garrulous in a café:
Each is a charmed ape. The truth becomes a cage
For trapped excitements. "He suspects I have a lover!";
"You must take care"; "She can't sink any lower!"

Yes, it's the telling not the tale. The box
Rifled, look at that smile on the face of the fat boy
As he passes in the corridor the most hated master
In the school. What does he know? It doesn't matter.
It's who he tells. Not his baby-sister,
But someone to charm. Perhaps the baby-sitter,
Curled up with *Cosmopolitan* and a lacy
Thigh, who will sit up and take it like a lady.

God knows, we all like secrets in small doses,
But beware. If she tells you whom she dotes
On, you're next. And maybe you're a blurter,
Your whole world revelation and bluster?
Who's your confidante, then? What is it makes
You spill the beans to her? It must be the male's
Need for approval; to charm. Or out of the blue
That mother ape. Is it? I haven't a clue.

# Amazing

So many numbered tracts,
So many pictured acts
And unexpected facts
    Saw I never;
So many bedroom arts,
So many private parts
And so few affected hearts
    Saw I never.

Such hiding and showing,
Such coming and going,
Such ahing and ohing
    Saw I never;
So many jobs for the hands
And explored hinterlands,
So many well-used glands
    Saw I never.

So many genuflections
Before soft erections,
So many false affections
    Saw I never;
So much thrashing and snorting,
So much fruitless exhorting
And such sad consorting
    Saw I never.

So little forbidden
To the bedridden,
So little hidden
    Saw I never;
So many immersions
In corrupt versions,
Such cheap excursions
    Saw I never.

Such drooping and dragging,
Such feinting and flagging,
Such sighing and sagging
    Saw I never;
So many waves and handstands
At cheering grandstands
And thumping bandstands
    Saw I never.

So many hopeless triers,
So many falsifiers,
So many downright liars
    Saw I never;
Such long thrasonical
And unironical
Erotic chronicle
    Saw I never.

So many greetings
And frequent meetings,
Such silent entreatings
    Saw I never.
So many on the brink
Of the fourth or fifth drink
Wasting their love in ink
    Saw I never.

# Words

Tongue is surface, too, though hidden.
Talking is an act, though hated.
Hands are still that would be moving
Over and over, but in silence.

Words are meeting, perhaps, though mistaken.
Lips are doorways, though on chains.
Heads are tilted, as before kissing
Over and over, but in silence.

Touch is withheld, often, though wanted.
Language claims lives, though wasted.
Eyes do much that the body would do
Over and over, but in silence.

# Linda

## 1

Linda, Linda, slender and pretty,
Biscuit girl in a biscuit city,
Packing the biscuits in paper boxes,
What do you dream of? How do you dream?
The cutters rise and fall and rise and cut
The chocolate, the coconut,
The Orange Princess and the Gypsy Cream.
The biscuits gather and the boxes shut,
But things are never what they seem.

In the school the bells are ringing,
In the playground girls are singing:
> *Lily, paper, hard-boiled eggs,*
> *Mr Swain has bandy legs.*
Linda, Linda, rude and sweet,
Skipping girl in a skipping street,
Singing and skipping all summer long:
> *Worms in the classroom, worms in the hall,*
> *Mr Swain will eat them all.*

The cutters fall and rise and fall
And biscuits are unending like a wall
And school is over and the summer's dream.


## 2

The day the sun invented flowers again
Her heart unfolded with the spring.
Paul had appeared and nothing was the same.

> *The railway's on its sleepers,*
> *The river's in its bed,*
> *All Berkshire is beneath us and*
> *The sky is overhead.*

Linda crossed the platform to the train.
Her warm little mouth reached up to his
And kissed and whispered his exciting name.

*What was it like before we met?*
*What did we ever do?*
*Can't think of anything like it*
*Or anyone like you.*

Weaving fingers find out that they fit
And all the secret pleasures they commit
Are like the touch of flowers in the rain.

3
A whistle from the primus:
The water's nice and hot.
I've got the milk and sugar
And teabags in the pot.
Sometimes there are sandwiches
And sometimes there are not,
But fishing is a fiddle
And Paul requires his tea.
He hasn't time to make it
So he leaves it all to me,
And there are always biscuits
(I bring along the tin.
I think it might be useful
To put the fishes in).
Fishing on the island, only me and him,
Fishing on the island all the afternoon,
The river flowing by us, full to the brim,
And the fishing is over all too soon.

When I packed the basket
Was there something I forgot?
It says *Plum* on the label
And Paul likes apricot.
I usually forget things
Though sometimes I do not,
But fishing is a fiddle
And Paul requires his tea.
He hasn't time to make it
So he leaves it all to me,
And there are always biscuits
(I bring along the tin.
I think it might be useful
To put the fishes in).
Fishing on the island, only me and him,
Fishing on the island all the afternoon,
The river flowing by us, full to the brim,
And the fishing is over all too soon.

The river's full of fishes.
You'd think he'd catch a lot.
I'll call out: "Have you got one?"
And Paul will answer: "What?"
Sometimes he will land one
And most times he will not,
But fishing is a fiddle
And Paul requires his tea,
And when his basket's empty
He holds it out to me
And grins to say he's sorry
(I love that silly grin
And I find it very useful
To put my kisses in).
Kissing on the island, only me and him,
Kissing on the island all the afternoon,
The river flowing by us, full to the brim,
And the kissing is over all too soon.

4

When we went down to Maidenhead
Paul had his clarinet.
I tried to do the steering and
We both got very wet.
But how he blew that liquorice stick!
The music on a thread
Rose like a nest of rooks above
His black and curly head.

> There's a rookery at Dorney
> But all the rooks have gone,
> Flapping their wings like overcoats
> They're struggling to put on.
> I love their wild black music,
> But all the rooks have gone.

We took a tent and Mum was mad.
Paul had his clarinet.
I had this spoon and china mug:
We made a fine duet.
But how he blew that wooden throat
Like a musical millionaire!
The black night-sound inside forced out
In squiggles on the air.

> There's a rookery at Dorney
> But all the rooks have gone,
> And clouds blow over empty trees
> Where once the summer shone,
> And Paul and his black music
> And all his love, have gone.

5
Linda went out in her wedges.
The day was average,
And masses of water were moving
Under Caversham Bridge.

Paul had promised to meet her
And take her on the river.
She looked again at her wristwatch
And gave a little shiver.

Well, wasn't he worth forgiving?
The hour ticked slowly on,
And she threw her Wrigley paper
Down at a frowning swan.

Several boys passed by her
And all of them managed to stare.
But Linda looked right through them
As if she didn't care.

You believe him if he tells you.
You think he's ever so nice
And it's hard to find he can never
Say the same thing twice.

Promises break like biscuits.
Nothing keeps for ever.
But time runs on and on and on,
Deep as the lying river.

6
Linda, Linda, older and wiser,
Far from childhood in a biscuit town,
Making biscuits where the Thames winds down,
Under the eyes of the supervisor,
Under the hands of the factory clock:

    Tick, tick, tick, tick,
      Crisp and crumbly, thin and thick.
The cutters rise and fall and rise,
Cutting out (surprise, surprise)
The chocolate, the coconut,
The Orange Princess and the Gypsy Cream.

But things are never what they seem.
The trains pass clanking on the track,
Distinct and jewelled in the quiet night:
    Tick, tick, tick, tick,
      In life's absurd arithmetic.
And Linda in the tunnel of her dream
All night is restless, staring back
As wisps of the dragon drift into the wind
And, smaller and smaller, Paul is waving,
Smaller and smaller, Paul is standing there.
And Linda dreams and dreams and dreams
Under the hands of the bedside clock,
Till bacon smells are in the air
And combs tug sleepily through morning hair
And nothing is ever what it seems.

## Valentine

The things about you I appreciate
    May seem indelicate:
I'd like to find you in the shower
And chase the soap for half an hour.
I'd like to have you in my power
    And see your eyes dilate.
I'd like to have your back to scour
And other parts to lubricate.
Sometimes I feel it is my fate
To chase you screaming up a tower
    Or make you cower
By asking you to differentiate
    Nietzsche from Schopenhauer.
I'd like successfully to guess your weight
    And win you at a fête.
I'd like to offer you a flower.

I like the hair upon your shoulders,
Falling like water over boulders.
I like the shoulders, too: they are essential.
Your collar-bones have great potential
(I'd like all your particulars in folders
    Marked *Confidential*).

I like your cheeks, I like your nose,
I like the way your lips disclose
The neat arrangement of your teeth
(Half above and half beneath)
    In rows.

I like your eyes, I like their fringes.
The way they focus on me gives me twinges.
Your upper arms drive me berserk.
I like the way your elbows work,
    On hinges.

I like your wrists, I like your glands,
I like the fingers on your hands.
I'd like to teach them how to count,
And certain things we might exchange,
Something familiar for something strange.
I'd like to give you just the right amount
  And get some change.

I like it when you tilt your cheek up.
I like the way you nod and hold a teacup.
I like your legs when you unwind them.
Even in trousers I don't mind them.
I like each softly-moulded kneecap.
I like the little crease behind them.
I'd always know, without a recap,
  Where to find them.

I like the sculpture of your ears.
I like the way your profile disappears
Whenever you decide to turn and face me.
I'd like to cross two hemispheres
  And have you chase me.
I'd like to smuggle you across frontiers
Or sail with you at night into Tangiers.
  I'd like you to embrace me.

I'd like to see you ironing your skirt
  And cancelling other dates.
I'd like to button up your shirt.
I like the way your chest inflates.
I'd like to soothe you when you're hurt
Or frightened senseless by invert-
   ebrates.

I'd like you even if you were malign
And had a yen for sudden homicide.
I'd let you put insecticide
    Into my wine.
I'd even like you if you were the Bride
    Of Frankenstein
Or something ghoulish out of Mamoulian's
    *Jekyll and Hyde.*
I'd even like you as my Julian
Of Norwich or Cathleen ni Houlihan.
    How melodramatic
If you were something muttering in attics
Like Mrs Rochester or a student of Boolean
    Mathematics.

You are the end of self-abuse.
You are the eternal feminine.
I'd like to find a good excuse
To call on you and find you in.
I'd like to put my hand beneath your chin,
    And see you grin.
I'd like to taste your Charlotte Russe,
I'd like to feel my lips upon your skin,
I'd like to make you reproduce.

I'd like you in my confidence.
I'd like to be your second look.
I'd like to let you try the French Defence
    And mate you with my rook.
I'd like to be your preference
    And hence
I'd like to be around when you unhook.
I'd like to be your only audience,
The final name in your appointment book,
    Your future tense.

## Practical Alice

The warnings went unheeded
    That sounded from the heart.
We rarely wondered whether
    We might remain apart:
It seemed that what was needed
Was just to be together.

I swore the tender jargon
    Would never pass my lips
Nor eyes be bright with pleasure
    When talking came to grips.
I drove a cruel bargain.
I took you at my leisure.

The strain of meeting faces
    Broke in a kiss and charmed
A circle I could enter
    And hope to leave unharmed.
You walked with giant paces
About that silent centre.

I lost you when you travelled,
    Moving a shade too fast.
The fashion was for lighter
    Stuff, never made to last,
And as the thread unravelled
I drew the garment tighter.

I suffered your attentions
    But somehow never could
Unearth my finer feelings
    To find out where we stood.
I stared at lots of ceilings
With lots of good intentions.

To please your casual hunger
    I only had to try
To melt when you grew colder
    As the packed months went by.
You did not wish me younger.
I scarcely wished you older.

Though parting is a nuisance
    It's clear we'll never stay
Close as the fatal minute
    That ticked our lives away.
And now the handclasp loosens
And feels the space within it.

## How Many Goodly Creatures

When freshmen have thoughts of adoring
    And tutors are keen to impress,
When the wife of the provost starts pouring
    And the chaplain begins to confess,
When the poet has hopes of reciting
    And the wine buff sets out to unscrew
Who is it they think of inviting?
    Miranda, my dear, it is you.

When scramblers open the throttle
    And choristers open their lips,
When committees discuss a new bottle
    And scholars observe an eclipse,
When candidates come to negotiate
    And christians lay tea-cups for two
With whom would they rather associate?
    Miranda, my dear, it is you.

Whenever they call and can't find you
    You have to reveal where you've been,
And when they come round again (mind you,
    You'll always arrange to be in)
You explain why it is you can't meet them
    And doggedly talk the thing through.
If anyone hated to cheat them,
    Miranda, my dear, it is you.

When quarter-backs have to give quarter,
    When forwards fall back, when the eight
Steps not in the shell but the water
    And the master refuses a gate,
When the scrum-half sees none of the action
    And the wrists of the slips turn to glue,
What's proved to be such a distraction?
    Miranda, my dear, it is you.

But everyone knows he's a rival
    (They're queuing three deep at your door)
And no one has hopes of survival
    Or ways of increasing his score
Unless you have given your blessing
    Do they know if you have? Not a clue.
Who's happy to keep them all guessing?
    Miranda, my dear, it is you.

Classicists love the Acropolis,
    Lawyers are crazy for torts,
Economists value monopolies,
    Philosophers cherish their thoughts,
Eng-Litters are deep into drama
    And chemists are hot for a Blue,
But what is it punctures their armour?
    Miranda, my dear, it is you.

Donald has asked you to dinner,
    There's a party with Denis at six,
Here's Dave pedalled up on his spinner,
    The Peugeot that's waiting is Dick's.
By the end of the evening you're woozy,
    But still your admirers pursue.
If ever a girl wasn't choosy,
    Miranda, my dear, it is you.

When Adrian writes you a letter
    You send a delightful reply,
If Rodney complains he's no better
    You never suspect it's a lie,
When William weeps on your shoulder
    You notice his brand of shampoo;
If anyone wished they were older,
    Miranda, my dear, it is you.

Whose partings were never as tragic
    As second-year rumours alleged?
Whose drawers are full of Black Magic?
    Whose RSVPs are gilt-edged?
Who lists all her friends in her diary
    With a detailed dispassionate view
Like a clerk in a public enquiry?
    Miranda, my dear, it is you.

## Examination

The wasted roses droop from stems
Defying time like lowered hems
    And legs tucked under.
The frowning beauty in a rage
Darkens the problematic page
    Like June thunder.

Could time restore what scribbles fail
Upon the sheet to make less pale
    What pure idea
Might send its fragrance out upon
The deadening oblivion
    She feels is near?

Three times one falling hand defines
The figured circle that confines
    Her inspiration
As racing sentences unlock
The startling secrets which might mock
    Its cruel notation.

The uprights regular at first
Join with her loops like rhymes in verse
    But slowly worsen
As she plucks out of agony
A flowering sensibility
    In the third person.

And petals fall like falling souls
From the bright hope of button-holes
    On beating hearts
Or like those fragile, half-grotesque
And crumpled papers on the desk,
    Her false starts.

Time after all has nothing left
And like a spendthrift after theft
    Of what for years
Was wildly longed-for in a lover's
Waking dream, she soon discovers
    Her prize is tears.

Now the examination room
Is empty of both girl and bloom
    And who would think
That so much effort had been spent
On this small part of what she meant
    In so much ink?

## Gone to Ground

Veuve du Vernay in the gutter, flattened wire and querns of
                                                          cork
Mark where candidates vacated (like the elders of the Kirk
Joining in a witches' rout) the holy temple of their rites —
Schola Magna Borealis — spilling gowned inebriates.
Prior to every paper, files of desks were sown with writing-
                                                          books
Germinating inkily beneath the working rows of backs;
Pentels played superbly in the cradles of their moving fists;
Silent whispers to the ceiling charmed the peacocks, prayed for
                                                          Firsts;
Fingers propped up profiles Buonarroti might have liked to
                                                          carve;
Unimaginable beauties shut in pallor like a cave
On a friendly surface flowers and antihistamines had made
Brought to life the latent heroines of *My Last Duchess, Maud,*
Nineteenth century victims of the poet's urge to wield his
                                                          power
Over girls not fully understood, bold, self-possessed though pure
(When their knowledge faltered, Kleenex, sweets and mascots
                                                          were employed).
Schools became a theatre where the memory and passion
                                                          played,
Empty all the summer once the fustian black and white had
                                                          gone
(Tennyson and Browning are allowed to lie unread again).
Down the High Street stroll unhindered naked knees and tartan
                                                          paunch,
Cluny's closed and Honey's empty save for someone buying
                                                          *Punch.*
All the mysteries enacted now are commonplace once more,
Sacred circumstances simply something travellers can admire.
Evidence is trapped unnoticed in the omnipresent lens:
Businessmen from Nagasaki freeze as one of them aligns
What remains of Magdalen Tower with an antiseptic grin,
CANDY underfoot and to the right a door of brass and green.

On the other corner Oxford Travel Agents are relieved:
Sheaves of booking stubs reveal where students' lives are now
being lived.
Transalpino, Apex, Eurotrain and private bus convey
Heart-struck, star-crossed, shattered souls to gaze upon a
different view.
Foreign cities heal with culture wounds that culture has
induced,
Love forgotten as the banger jolts through fascinating dust.
Soppy sentimental disconnected drainpipes go their ways,
Finding in a summer's absence much inducement to be wise.
Term was going out to dinner, giving bear-hugs in the quad,
Heads together over just the quantity of work required.
Literature is what you make it and it's bound to turn to tears.
Now it's nature's turn to comfort as the dear ideal retires:
Thumbs along the autostrada bring an everchanging view;
Tents in Sligo echo with the savage wounding of a vow.
Human lineaments will alter since you make them what they
seem;
Rocks and water are unyielding for their substance is the same.
Wordsworth told us once and we were almost willing to believe
(Keeping fingers crossed behind our back because we knew
that love
Conquered after all each famous effort to be understood,
Offering the various shapes of dull eternity instead).
Passion doesn't bear examination — though perhaps it should,
Shaping as it does the source from which all mental life is shed.
Ardent alpha-minus and besotted beta-plus, God knows,
Can't be much preferred to grieving gamma, narcissist NS,
Given our agreement on the joy of unrequited love,
Caring only that its fatal feelings may be kept alive,
Never to be disappointed by their hope of being fulfilled
Like a conjuror's spectators who are eager to stay fooled.
Don't expect a tutor to stay moping in a tourist town:
Bright at the receiver you will only hear the dialling tone.
If you're passing through yourself, perhaps to bring me back
some books
(Quantities I lent you: won't you need to put them in a box?)

Don't imagine I'll be waiting, kettle steaming, on the hour.
*Did* you call? I'm sorry! I'm afraid that's just the way things
                                                    are.
Was my room locked and the tap not dripping, friendly, on
                                              the stair?
Did the scout look blank and turn away and give her tea a
                                                    stir?
Did you interrupt the Lodge's cricket, stamp and tear your
                                                    hair?
Hearing Strutt recite his lesson: "Mr Fuller is not here,
Having taken up a new appointment as the top masseur
(Being handy, tender, ready, when the nape and hips are sore)
With the Russian women's swimming, pole-vault and gymnastic
                                                    teams,
Keen, you see, on sport and travel when he isn't keeping
                                                    terms.
Leave a message with the porter? Always happy to oblige.
Got a packet for him, have you? Hope it isn't very large.
Look, his pigeon-hole is full already: invitations, cheques,
Magazines and scented envelopes as soft as ladies' cheeks.
Come back in October (what's the phrase? — 'the sere and
                                              yellow leaf').
Michaelmas, I'm sure, will see us all resuming normal life."
Life! Ah, life, who always lives us so intensely at his will;
Life in lying chapters, promising that things will soon be well;
Life, who understands us all but keeps the secret in his book;
Life, the truest friend — who, once he goes away, will not
                                              come back.

## The College Ghost

*For Hugh Sinclair*

At 11.25, after a college beano
Designed to wish a retiring colleague well
(Who with a glass in one hand, a watch in the other
Like the pieces of Alice's mushroom, sat and then rose
To remind with smiling words why we shall miss him),

At that suspended hour of a summer night,
Having made my few farewells, collected my gown,
My black tie carelessly telling the approximate time,
The claret filling my toes, the toes my shoes
And the shoes knowing more or less the way to go,

I left the smoking-room and paced the cloisters
In the wrong direction, almost three sides where one
Would do, to find the passage to take me safely
To the only place where we regularly fall
Utterly unconscious without rebuke or danger

And came at once upon the college ghost
Lolling in a Gothic arch not far from the kitchens.
It had a gross nonchalant air, pretending
That it simply chanced to be there waiting for no one
Particularly, picking its non-existent nails.

Its face was puffy and indistinct, the eyes
Burnt holes, nose gone, the grin healthy
But upside down. It wore a college scarf
And a row of pens in its shroud like a boffin,
Slouched in its window in a May Week pose.

It watched me as I approached and it made its greeting,
Not deferent, not assertive, simply assuming
Its right to expect me to stop, as though our notes
Had crossed and whatever it was had there and then
To be settled and some confusion straightened out.

The night was dark and winy as a cellar,
The only noises the clacking of the flagpole
On St Swithun's tower and the thumping of my heart.
But I wasn't surprised. I felt it was an encounter
Fated at one or another time to occur.

I fingered the keys in my pocket, the inner and outer
Circuits, comforting brass and heavy for turning
The secret doors and great gates of the college,
Fingered them as though they were amulets
To keep at a distance the presence I found before me.

Behind and through it gleamed the broad green square
Of the lawn where all that summer afternoon
In various attitudes of conversation
Undergraduates had sat with early teas
Outlapping the lingering remains of lunch

And the voice of the shapeless shape, if voice it was,
Drifted towards me softly, catching my ear
Exactly like a carefully-placed loudspeaker,
And its words were the words of all who had sat on that lawn
Through similar afternoons until such darkness fell:

"Though I am not often seen here, at least at times
When troublesome tasks last through daylight or take
You from page to page of assorted memoranda,
Nose down like a broker or a winded traveller
Frantic for the last train in a foreign city,

"Though I am discrepant and uncorroborated
As a reputation; embarrassing as the memory
Of insufficient words at parting; feared
Like a summons for a forgotten misdemeanour;
Still, I do appear, and appear to you now.

"It's precisely at times like this, when you are distracted
By well-being and owl-light from shutting your senses
To what I represent and am ready to communicate
That I eagerly seize my chance to materialize
Like an image on paper in a paddled tray.

"You reckon you can shortly make your escape,
Say more next time. So be it. That is your manner.
But for the moment, stay. I have something to tell you
That has been keeping but will not keep for ever,
Like Clipsham stone or a Pomerol, but not so nice.

"It concerns the conspiracy to keep me partly asleep
With promise of distinct pleasures belonging to
The forms of success towards which you propelled me,
Wise like an elder framing a constitution
Before he retires and dies a powerless legend.

"You gave me much that could not shame the giver
Whatever whoops of joy and sounds of breakage
Greeted your smiles, fond as a distant uncle,
When the package was ripped open, the contents spilled,
The crucial instructions immediately lost.

"But grammar burned bishops and nations fell to the prism.
I negotiated the quantities of blood required
To put into effect the decrees of the Ineffable.
I argued over heads that I knew were soon
To lose all interest in what they commandeered.

"I was present when the planet first took its header
Into the bracing briny of the impermanent.
I dignified the scribbled with the spacing of nuts and muttons.
I bowed in Washington, once the place was invented.
Through me the Greeks discovered Australia.

"Theories of diet dispersed tribes, infections
Accompanied stately truths like interpreters.
I took your towers for wit, your lawns for sorrow,
And made the friendships that reduced brown acres
Of imposing mahogany to the space of a handclasp.

"Even when the world in a more appealing tongue
Spoke of the price to be paid for a share of power,
It was to you I referred with a slight shrug
And perhaps a mock self-deprecatory grin
That could not decide if it cared for your approval.

"You gave it. And that was when I became a ghost,
Rioting invisibly in the halls and staircases
Of my consecrated youth, while everything true
And good fell from my fingers or from windows,
Drifting like laughter in the direction of the ivy.

"Now I appear to you because at last
I have rejoined you for ever. Life has made
Its choice. My affairs are finally quite complete
And there is nothing left in the world to alter.
Whatever you teach will make no difference at all."

So saying, it boyishly scissored the stone sill
With a careless stretch of the arms and a hint of flannel
As the bells in the tower tensed to tell three quarters
And the moon behaved as it likes to do at these moments,
Nodding above the treescape like an impresario.

Which way it went I really couldn't say,
But it had gone. And so I slowly continued
My right-angled path through the heart of the college,
Less light of foot, but somewhat enlightened,
Slightly unsure of what I thought I had heard.

Darkness was all around me like a sixth
Sense, or the absolute quiet of certain music
That the hand trembles to play. And it was like
The world pressing on its pockets of resistance.
Like righteous claims of love. Or threats of war.

And indeed, I thought, the ultimate chaos will surely be
A predicate of just this irresponsible architecture
Of convinced laws and prayers that meddled for years
With the best of fateful intentions until the wind changed.
The words were in my head like an egg in a bottle.

Thoughts too late to unthink: I had the feeling
Of being betrayed by something of my choosing,
Something I had connived at, something belonging
To the projection of a long-suspected failing,
Haunted by the forces it exploits.